TABLE OF CONTENTS

NEW YEAR'S DAY

In the United States, Canada, Europe, Australia, and other countries, New Year's Day is celebrated on January 1 of each year. The day before New Year's Day is referred to as New Year's Eve. As the clock strikes midnight on New Year's Eve, people blow noisemakers and whistles, dance, enjoy parties and fireworks, and sing the song "Auld Lang Syne" to welcome the new year.

Other countries and cultures also celebrate the arrival of the New Year. Chinese New Year is an important celebration in late January or early February. The Jewish New Year, Rosh Hashanah, is usually celebrated in September. (See pages 57-59 for Rosh Hashanah.)

New Year's Eve Party Hat

Things you will need
- Construction paper
- Yarn or string
- Clear tape
- Crayons or markers
- Scissors

What to do

1. Roll a large piece of construction paper into a cone shape and trim the excess.

2. Unroll the cone and decorate the construction paper with crayons or markers.

3. Roll the construction paper back into a cone with the decorations on the outside. Tape the sides of the construction paper together to form a cone-shaped hat.

4. Tape a piece of yarn or string on the inside of each side of the completed hat to use as a chin strap.

2

Glitter Picture

Things you will need
- Construction paper
- Glitter
- Glue
- Crayons or markers

What to do

1. Write "Happy New Year" on the construction paper with markers or crayons.

2. Draw noisemakers, streamers, confetti, or other New Year's items on the paper.

3. Write the year on the sign with glue.

4. While the glue is still wet, carefully sprinkle glitter over the glue and shake off the excess glitter into a trash can.

5. Allow the glue to dry completely.

Fireworks

Things you will need
- White construction paper
- Red, yellow, or orange crayon, and black crayons
- Coin

What to do

1. Cover a piece of white construction paper with a heavy layer of red, yellow, or orange crayon.

2. Cover the same area with a heavy layer of black crayon.

3. Using the edge of a coin, scratch a firework pattern and the year into the black crayon layer so the bright color shows through.

MARTIN LUTHER KING, JR., DAY

Dr. Martin Luther King, Jr. was a civil rights leader and Baptist minister born in Atlanta, Georgia in 1929. Dr. King led peaceful protests and gave speeches in an attempt to bring equal rights to African-Americans. He received the Nobel Peace Prize in 1964. In 1968, he was killed in Memphis, Tennessee. Martin Luther King, Jr., Day was made a holiday in 1983.

Human Chain

Things you will need

- Human shape pattern (page 6)
- White construction paper
- Brown, black, yellow, and orange yarn
- Glue
- Clear tape
- Crayons and markers
- Scissors

What to do

* Teacher: Enlarge the human shape pattern onto white construction paper.

1. Cut out the pattern and color it as a self-portrait.

2. Cut several pieces of yarn and glue them to the pattern for hair.

3. Have the students help tape the decorated patterns hand-to-hand, like a paper doll chain.

* Display the completed chain on a bulletin board with a quotation from King's "I Have A Dream" speech (see page 5).

Our Dreams

Things you will need
- Cloud and Dr. King patterns (page 6)
- White construction paper
- Sky-blue bulletin board paper
- Crayons and markers
- Scissors

> I have a dream that my four little children will one day live in a nation where they will not be judged by the color of their skin but by the content of their character.
>
> – Dr. Martin Luther King, Jr.

What to do

* Teacher: Talk with the children about Dr. King's accomplishments and beliefs. Discuss what students can do to carry on Dr. King's dream (see above).

* Enlarge the cloud pattern on white construction paper.

* Cover a bulletin board with sky-blue paper. Enlarge and color the Dr. King pattern and place it in the center of the bulletin board.

* Make a thought bubble and write "I have a dream . . . " in the bubble. Place the bubble on the bulletin board above Dr. King.

1. Draw a picture on the cloud pattern to illustrate what Dr. King's dream means to the student and cut out the pattern.

2. Have students help add the completed cloud patterns to the bulletin board.

GROUNDHOG DAY

Every February 2, Groundhog Day, the groundhog becomes a weather forecaster. According to an old American legend, if the sun is shining on February 2 when the groundhog comes out of the hole or burrow to look for food, the groundhog will see his shadow, meaning there will be six more weeks of cold winter weather. If the sky is cloudy and the groundhog does not see his shadow, spring will arrive soon.

Peek-a-Boo Groundhog

Things you will need
- Groundhog torso pattern (page 9)
- Brown and black construction paper
- Large craft stick
- Glue
- Scissors

What to do

* Teacher: Copy the groundhog torso pattern on brown construction paper.

1. Cut out the groundhog and glue it to a large craft stick (see diagram).

2. Cut out an oval "groundhog hole" from black construction paper. Fold the oval in half widthwise and cut a slit in the burrow large enough for the groundhog pattern to slide through (see diagram).

3. Slide the groundhog up through the hole. Allow the student to pretend the groundhog is coming out of and going back in the hole.

Furry Pal

Things you will need
- Groundhog profile pattern (page 9)
- Brown and white construction paper
- Brown yarn
- Crayons
- Glue
- Scissors

What to do

* Teacher: Copy the groundhog profile on brown construction paper.

1. Cut out the groundhog and glue it to white construction paper.

2. Cut several lengths of brown yarn and glue them to the groundhog pattern to look like fur.

3. Complete the picture by adding grass, clouds, etc.

Shadow Play

Things you will need
- Groundhog profile pattern (page 9)
- Brown and black construction paper

What to do

* Teacher: Copy the groundhog pattern on brown construction paper.

* Enlarge the groundhog pattern 2-3 times larger than the original. Trace the enlarged pattern on black paper and cut out the profile shape.

* Use the two copies to demonstrate for the students why the groundhog might be afraid of his own shadow, as in the diagram above.

Groundhog Day Patterns

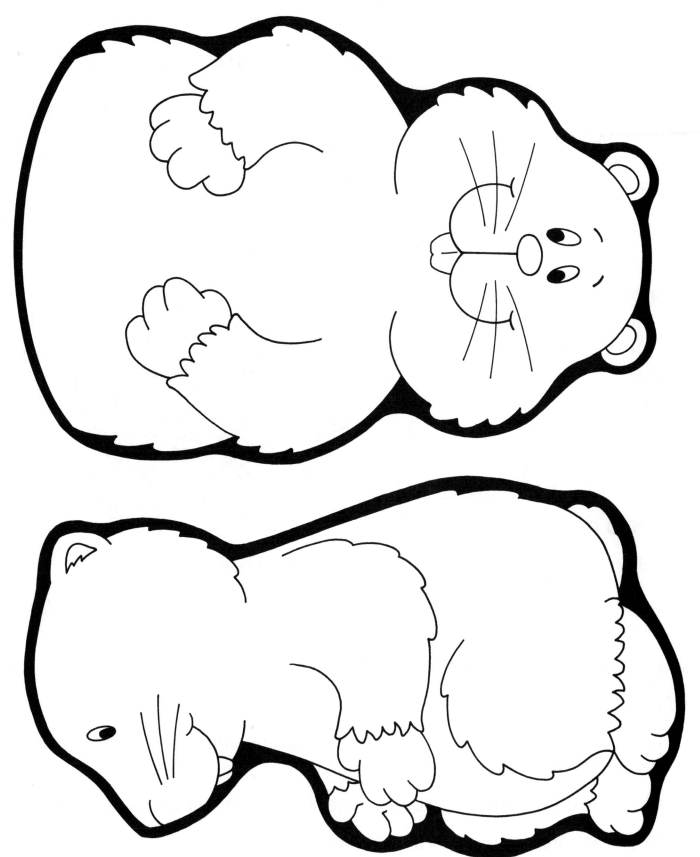

VALENTINE'S DAY

Valentine's Day is celebrated on February 14 by giving cards, candy, or flowers to loved ones and friends. Historical records suggest that Valentine's Day's association with love may have begun in several different ways. For example, early English records of Valentine's Day suggest that February 14 is the day on which birds choose their mates. The heart is used as a symbol for Valentine's Day because it represents love.

Heart Card

Things you will need

- Pink or red construction paper
- Pink, red, or white tissue paper
- Lace
- Glue
- Pencil
- Scissors

What to do

1. Fold a piece of pink or red construction paper in half.

2. Draw a heart on the folded construction paper about 8" wide and 6" long, leaving two flat sections along the top (see diagram).

3. Cut out the heart, leaving the two flat sections of the fold intact.

4. Draw a smaller heart shape on the heart.

5. Crumple small pieces of pink, red, or white tissue paper and glue the tissue paper pieces to cover the center of the heart.

6. Glue lace around the back edges of the card so that it shows from the front.

7. Open the card and write a Valentine message inside.

I Love You "Sew"

Things you will need
- Large heart pattern (page 15)
- Red or pink construction paper
- White yarn or ribbon, 36" long
- Markers
- Hole punch
- Scissors

What to do

* Teacher: Copy the heart pattern on red or pink construction paper

1. Cut out the heart.

2. Punch evenly-spaced holes around the heart's edge with a hole punch.

3. "Sew" around the heart's edge with white yarn or ribbon.

4. Tie a bow at the top of the heart.

5. Write a valentine message on the heart.

Heart Necklace

Things you will need
- Small heart pattern (page 15)
- Red or pink construction paper
- Ribbon
- Yarn
- Glue
- Hole punch
- Scissors

What to do

* Teacher: Copy the small heart pattern on red or pink construction paper.

1. Cut out the heart.

2. Tie a small ribbon into a bow and glue it to the heart.

3. Punch a hole in the heart with a hole punch. Tie a piece of yarn through the hole. Make sure the yarn is long enough to fit safely over the child's head.

4. Wear the necklace on Valentine's Day.

Pom Pom Heart

Things you will need
- Large heart pattern (page 15)
- Tagboard
- Red pom poms
- Lace
- Glue
- Scissors

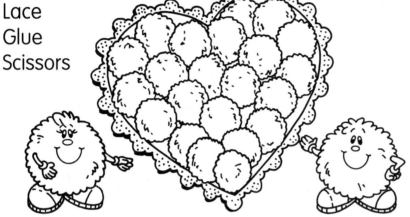

What to do

1. Using the heart pattern, cut out a large heart from tagboard.

2. Glue red pom poms on the tagboard heart to cover the shape completely.

3. Glue lace around the back edges, so that it is visible from the front.

Hearts on Ribbon

Things you will need
- Wallpaper scraps with different patterns
- Yarn
- Ribbon, 10" x ¹/₂"
- Glue
- Stapler and staples
- Scissors

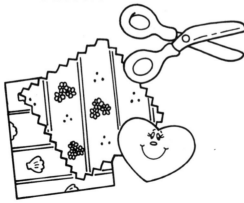

What to do

1. Cut out three different sized hearts from wallpaper.

2. Tie three small yarn bows and glue one bow in the middle of each heart.

3. Space the hearts evenly apart and glue them to a piece of ribbon.

4. Loop the ribbon at the top and staple or glue it closed to make a hanger.

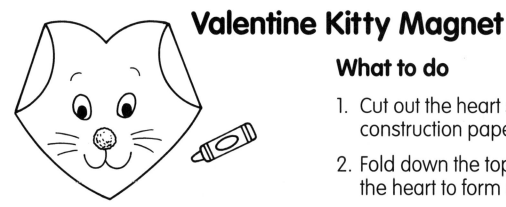

Valentine Kitty Magnet

What to do

1. Cut out the heart shape from white construction paper.

2. Fold down the top part of each side of the heart to form ears (see diagram).

3. Draw a cat face on the heart with markers or crayons and color the insides of the ears pink.

4. Glue on a black pom pom nose.

5. Attach a self-adhesive magnet to the back of the completed kitty.

Things you will need
- Large heart pattern (page 15)
- White construction paper
- Small black pom pom
- Self-adhesive magnet
- Markers or crayons
- Scissors

Valentine Mouse

Things you will need
- Large and small heart patterns (page 15)
- Gray and pink construction paper
- 2 small wiggly eyes
- 3 black pipe cleaners
- Tape
- Glue
- Scissors

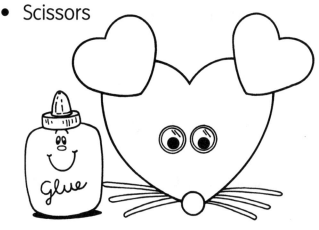

What to do

* Teacher: Copy the large and small heart patterns on gray construction paper.

1. Cut out the heart patterns.

2. Glue the small hearts to the large heart (as shown) to represent ears and a face.

3. Cut a small circle from pink construction paper for a nose and glue onto the point of the heart.

4. Glue on two wiggly eyes.

5. Tape pipe cleaners to the back of the valentine mouse for whiskers.

Heart Girls and Boys

Things you will need

- Large and small heart patterns (page 15)
- Red, pink, and white construction paper
- Pink yarn
- Glue
- Markers
- Scissors

What to do

* Teacher: Make two copies of the large heart on red construction paper. Copy 16 small hearts onto pink construction paper.

1. Cut out two large hearts for bodies.

2. Cut out 16 small pink hearts to make eyes, mouths, hands, feet, and a bow tie.

3. From white construction paper, cut four 1" x 6" strips for arms and four 1" x 11" strips for legs.

4. Fan-fold the strips.

5. Glue the 6" fan-folded strips to the large red hearts for arms and glue on the 11" fan-folded strips for legs. Glue a small heart to the end of each folded strip for hands and feet.

6. Glue small hearts to each large heart for eyes and a mouth.

7. To finish the girl heart, draw eyelashes. Then, tie a bow from pink yarn and glue the bow to the girl's head.

8. To finish the boy heart, glue two small hearts together point to point to make a bow tie, then glue the bow tie to the point of the boy heart.

Valentine's Day Patterns

15

VALENTINE'S DAY

PRESIDENTS' DAY

Presidents' Day is celebrated on the third Monday in February to honor Presidents George Washington and Abraham Lincoln.

George Washington was the first president of the United States. Legends say that as a boy, Washington chopped down a cherry tree and when asked about it said, "I cannot tell a lie," admitting his mistake.

Abraham Lincoln was the sixteenth president of the United States. He was called the Great Emancipator because he freed the slaves. Lincoln's boyhood home was a log cabin.

Log Cabin

Things you will need

- Log cabin pattern (page 18)
- Brown and light-colored construction paper
- Cotton balls
- Crayons or markers
- Glue
- Scissors

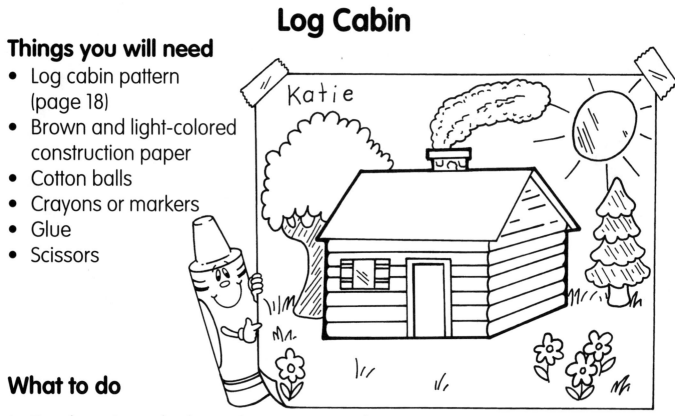

What to do

* Teacher: Copy the log cabin pattern on brown construction paper.

1. Cut out the log cabin.

2. Glue the log cabin to a piece of light-colored construction paper.

3. Using markers or crayons, add details like grass, trees, and the sun.

4. Glue stretched cotton balls to the top of chimney for smoke.

Cherry Tree

Things you will need

- Cherry tree pattern (page 19)
- Green construction paper
- Small red pom poms
- Glue
- Scissors

What to do

* Teacher: Enlarge two copies of the cherry tree pattern on green construction paper.

* Give each child two tree patterns and tell him a number between one and ten.

1. Cut out the cherry trees.

2. Write the numeral on one copy of the pattern. On the other copy of the pattern, glue the matching number of pom poms.

3. Have the students help display the completed Cherry Trees above the chalkboard or place them in a math center to practice matching the correct trees.

Presidents' Day Patterns

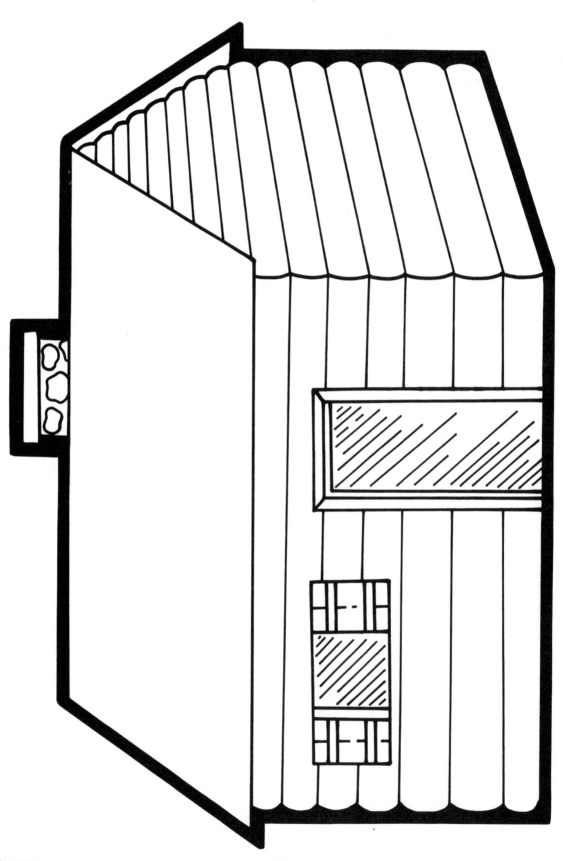

PRESIDENTS' DAY

MARDI GRAS

Mardi Gras, or Shrove Tuesday, is the last day of the period of festival before Ash Wednesday, which marks the beginning of Lent. Mardi Gras means "Fat Tuesday" in French.

The largest Mardi Gras celebration in the United States is held in New Orleans, Louisiana. During the Mardi Gras festival, people listen to dixieland jazz music, wear masks and costumes, watch parades, and go to parties and balls. During Mardi Gras parades, people on floats throw plastic bead necklaces and coins to parade watchers.

Mardi Gras Pasta Necklace

Things you will need
- Uncooked rigatoni and wagon wheel pasta
- Rubbing alcohol
- Resealable plastic bag
- Waxed paper
- Food coloring
- Yarn
- Scissors

What to do

* Teacher: Before the activity begins, dye the pasta bright colors. To dye pasta, place several drops of rubbing alcohol and food coloring in a plastic bag and shake the pasta until it is colored. Pour the colored pasta onto waxed paper and let it dry overnight. (Tell the children the pasta is not edible.)

* Cut a piece of yarn long enough to fit safely over the child's head.

1. String the yarn with various colors of wagon wheels or rigatoni.

2. After stringing as many pasta pieces as desired, tie the ends of the yarn together in a knot.

3. Wear the colorful necklace during Mardi Gras.

Mardi Gras Mask

Things you will need

- Mask pattern (at right)
- Tagboard
- Glitter, sequins, buttons, etc.
- Glue
- Masking tape
- Craft stick or dowel
- Scissors

What to do

1. Glue the mask pattern to tagboard and cut out.

2. Cut out the eye holes. Note: The size of the eye holes may need to be adjusted.

3. Decorate the mask with glitter, sequins, buttons, etc.

4. Tape a craft stick or dowel to the back of one side to use as a handle.

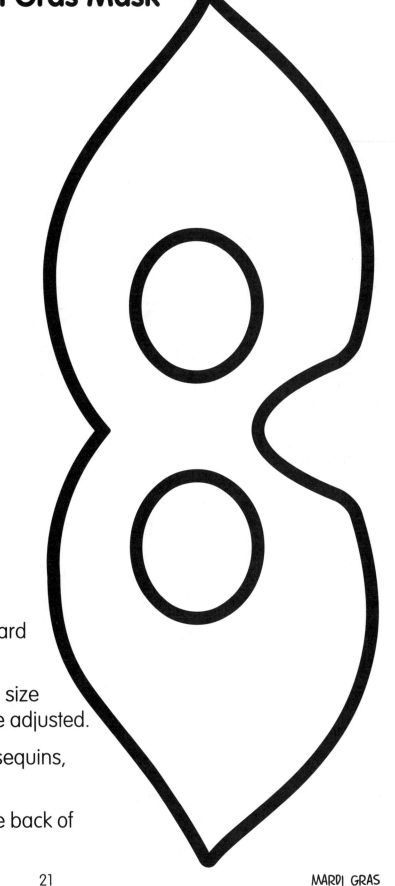

ST. PATRICK'S DAY

St. Patrick's Day is celebrated on March 17 in honor of St. Patrick, the patron saint of Ireland, who was a missionary to Ireland in the 400's.

In Ireland, St. Patrick's Day is primarily a religious holiday marked by religious services, community gatherings, and the wearing of shamrocks, a symbol of good luck.

In other countries, St. Patrick's Day is celebrated primarily as a nonreligious holiday. On this day, people often wear green clothing and attend parties and parades. The first St. Patrick's Day celebration in the United States took place in Boston, Massachusetts in 1737.

Shamrock Crown

Things you will need
- Shamrock pattern (page 24)
- Green construction paper
- Glue or tape
- Scissors

What to do

* Teacher: Cut a 2" wide strip of paper long enough to fit around a child's head with approximately 1" left at each end.

* Glue or tape the ends together to form a headband.

1. Using the pattern as a guide, cut out several shamrocks from green construction paper and glue the shamrocks around the headband to make a "crown."

Pot of Gold

Things you will need

- Pot of gold pattern (page 24)
- White construction paper
- Paintbrushes
- Watercolor paints
- Glue stick

What to do

1. Cut out and paint the pot of gold pattern.

2. Glue the pattern on one side of a piece of white construction paper.

3. Paint a rainbow which ends at the pot of gold.

Shamrock Garland

Things you will need

- Shamrock patterns (page 24)
- Green construction paper
- Tape
- Scissors

What to do

1. Fan-fold a piece of green construction paper into 4" folds.

2. Using the pattern, trace a shamrock on the fan-folded paper (with each side of the pattern overlapping a fold) and cut it out, being careful not to cut the fan-folds.

3. Have students help tape the completed garlands together to form one long garland.

St. Patrick's Day Patterns

PASSOVER

Passover, or "Pesach" in Hebrew, the oldest Jewish holiday, is celebrated for seven or eight days. It is a commemoration of the Jews' safe journey across the Red Sea during their escape from slavery in Egypt.

During Passover, only food which has been prepared in a special way can be eaten. The Seder, a meal at which the story of the Jews' Exodus from Egypt is told, takes place during the first two evenings of Passover. A special plate with ritual Seder food is placed on the table. An extra goblet, the "Cup of Elijah," is also placed on the table. The Seder plate contains food items which have special meanings. Parsley is a reminder of Jewish slaves' lack of food. It is dipped into salt water to symbolize the tears of the slaves. Parsley also represents spring and rebirth. Horseradish, a bitter root, is a reminder of Jewish slavery. Charoset is a mixture of apples, raisins, and nuts that represents the building mortar used by the slaves in Egypt. The egg symbolizes rebirth and new life. The bone represents the lamb offered to God by the Jews before their departure from Egypt.

At the Seder, matzo, a flat cracker like unleavened bread, is eaten as a reminder of the Jews' rushed escape, as there was no time to bake.

Matzo

Things you will need
- Light brown construction paper
- Brown yarn
- Hole punch
- Scissors

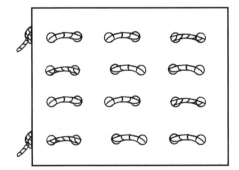

What to do

1. Fold a piece of light brown construction paper in half.

2. Punch two rows of six holes each in the folded paper.

3. Unfold the paper and weave the yarn in and out of the holes. Tie the yarn off at both ends.

Seder Plate

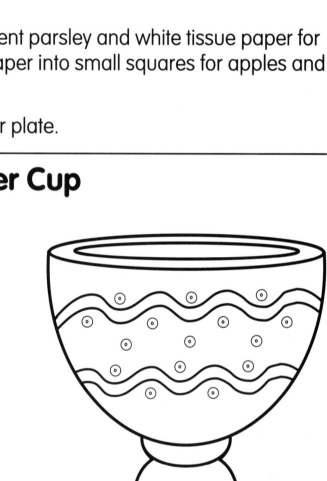

Things you will need
- Bone and egg patterns (page 27)
- Colorful paper plate
- White construction paper
- Green and white tissue paper
- Glue
- Scissors

What to do

1. Cut out the bone and egg patterns.

2. Crumple green tissue paper to represent parsley and white tissue paper for horseradish. Cut white construction paper into small squares for apples and almonds.

3. Glue all of the items to a colorful paper plate.

Passover Cup

Things you will need
- Passover cup pattern (page 27)
- White construction paper
- Aluminum foil, gold wrapping paper, etc.
- Ricrac, sequins, beads, etc.
- Markers and crayons
- Glue
- Scissors

What to do

1. Cut out the pattern.

2. Decorate the cup for Passover with foil, wrapping paper, beads, etc.

Passover Patterns

EASTER

Easter is a Christian holiday celebrating the resurrection of Jesus Christ. It occurs on the first Sunday after the full moon on or after March 21.

The name "Easter" is derived from "Eostre," the Anglo-Saxon goddess whose festival took place in the springtime.

In many countries, the egg and the white hare represent new life and rebirth and remind Christians of the resurrection of Christ.

Many Christians celebrate Easter by attending religious services, sharing family dinners, eating sweet treats, and participating in Easter egg hunts.

Cup Bunny

Things you will need
- Ear, eye, and feet patterns (page 33)
- Pink construction paper
- 2 small white bathroom cups
- Black permanent marker
- Cotton ball
- Glue
- Scissors

What to do

1. Cut out the eyes and ears. Color the centers of the ear patterns pink. Glue the eyes and ears to the cup.

2. Cut out a pink construction paper nose and glue it to the bottom of the head cup. Draw a mouth using a black marker.

3. Glue the feet pattern to the bottom of the second cup.

4. Glue on a cotton ball tail.

5. Glue two cups together as shown with the bunny-head cup on top. Allow the glue to dry.

Easter Bunny Puppet

Things you will need

- Bunny head pattern (page 34)
- Paper lunch bag
- Glue
- Crayons or markers
- Scissors

What to do

1. Cut out the bunny head pattern.

2. Color the bunny head.

3. Glue the bunny head to the bottom of the lunch bag (as shown).

Cotton Ball Lamb

Things you will need

- Large and small oval patterns (page 33)
- Tagboard
- Light-colored construction paper
- Cotton balls
- Glue
- Black washable stamp pad
- Black marker

What to do

* Teacher: Make tagboard templates of the large and small oval patterns for the lamb's body and head.

1. Trace the oval patterns on construction paper to make the lamb's body and head.

2. Press one finger on the black stamp pad and make four fingerprints for the lamb's feet.

3. Glue cotton balls on the large oval to make the lamb's wool.

4. On the small oval, draw a lamb's face with a black marker.

Chick Card

Things you will need

- Chick and egg shell patterns (page 35)
- Yellow and pastel construction paper
- Glue
- Markers
- Scissors

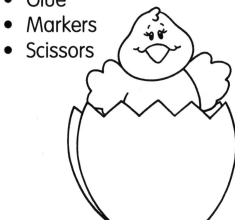

What to do

* Teacher: Copy the chick pattern on yellow construction paper.

1. Cut out the chick pattern and color the chick's beak orange.

2. Fold a piece of pastel construction paper in half. Trace the egg shell pattern on the folded paper with the straight part of the egg on the fold. Cut the egg out, being careful not to cut the fold.

3. Glue the chick to the <u>back</u> of the egg card so that the chick's head shows from the front.

4. Write a message below the chick.

Bunny Headband

What to do

* Teacher: To make a headband, wrap a strip of construction paper around the child's head, overlap it about 1", and tape the sides together.

1. Cut a small circle from the middle of a paper plate. Then, cut off the edges of the paper plate for ears (see diagram).

2. Color the centers of the ears pink and draw a bunny face on the circle.

3. Glue the ears to the back of the headband, facing forward. Glue the face to the front.

Things you will need

- Paper plate
- Pink construction paper
- Pink crayons or markers
- Clear tape
- Glue
- Scissors

Egg Basket

Things you will need
- Egg patterns (page 35)
- Paper plate
- Crayons or markers
- Glue
- Scissors

What to do

1. Cut a basket shape from a paper plate by cutting out the interior portion of the top half of the plate and leaving the entire rim intact.

2. Color and cut out several egg patterns.

3. Glue the eggs to the back of the basket so it looks "filled" with eggs.

Cross Necklace

Things you will need
- Construction paper or tagboard cut into four strips: 5" x 2", 4" x 1", 7" x 2", 6" x 1"
- Yarn or ribbon
- Glue
- Hole punch
- Scissors

What to do

1. Cut "Vs" in all ends of each strip.

2. Glue the 1" construction paper pieces to the middle of the 2" pieces. Glue all of the pieces together to form a cross shape.

3. Punch a hole at the top of the cross with a hole punch and string with yarn or ribbon for a necklace.

Shy Rabbit

Things you will need

- Basket and rabbit head patterns (below)
- Construction paper
- Index card, cut in half
- Craft stick
- Crayons or markers
- Glue
- Scissors

What to do

* Teacher: Enlarge the basket and rabbit head patterns.

1. Color and cut out the patterns.

2. Glue the rabbit head to the back of the basket (as shown).

3. Write "Happy Easter" on half an index card and glue a craft stick to the index card.

4. Glue the craft stick to the back of the basket (as shown).

Easter Patterns

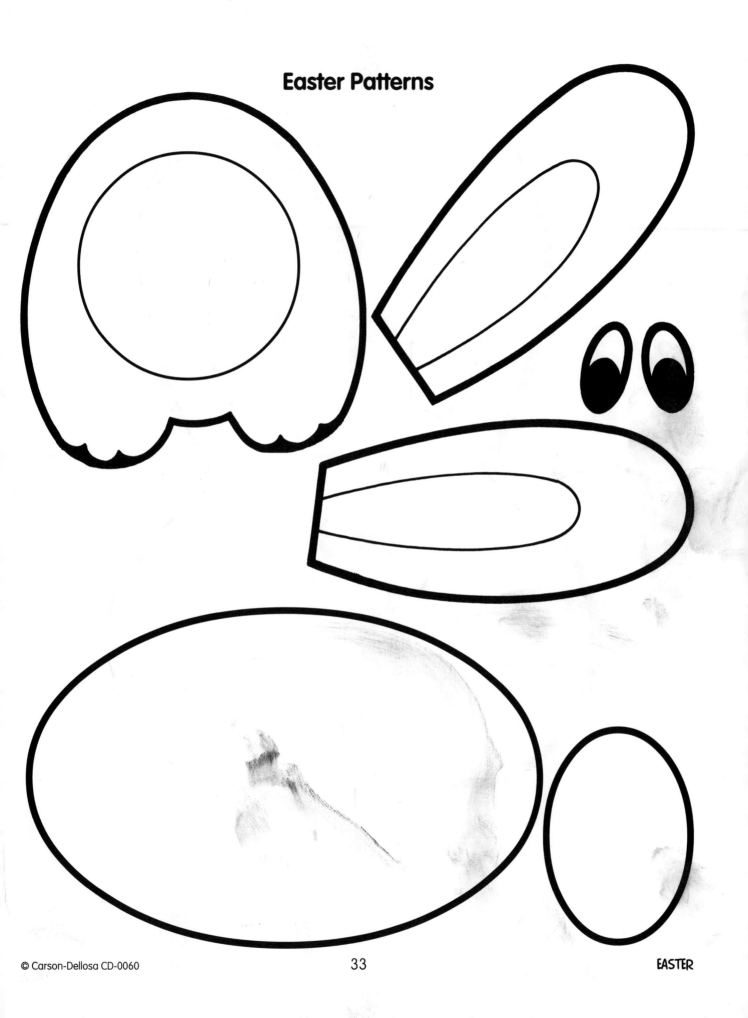

33

EASTER

34

Easter Patterns

EARTH DAY

Earth Day is not a designated holiday, but a time set aside in April to emphasize the importance of protecting and conserving our natural environment. The first Earth Day occurred on April 22, 1970 and was organized by Gaylord Nelson.

Earth Day is an international event marked by festivals and information fairs, community cleanup efforts, and grassroots demonstrations for environmental protection.

Peat Pot People

Things you will need
- 3" peat pot
- Potting soil
- Gravel
- Grass seed
- Water
- Construction paper scraps
- Glue
- Scissors

What to do

1. Cut out construction paper eyes, nose, and mouth and glue the pieces to a peat pot.

2. Fill the peat pot one-fourth full of gravel.

3. Fill the pot with soil, leaving $1/4$" at the top of the pot.

4. Sprinkle the soil with grass seed, then cover the seed with more soil.

5. Place the pot in a sunny place and water each day. After about a week, "hair" will begin to sprout. In about two weeks, the hair will be ready for a trim.

Earth Sponge Painting

Things you will need

- Sponges
- White butcher paper
- Green, brown, and blue tempera paint
- Pencil
- Scissors

What to do

* Teacher: Cut a large circle from white butcher paper for the class to paint.

* Draw continent shapes on the circle.

* Write the words "Our Earth" on a separate piece of butcher paper.

1. As a class, sponge paint the continents green and brown and the oceans blue.

2. Have the students help hang the completed earth and the "Our Earth" banner in the classroom.

MAY DAY

May Day occurs on May 1 and can be traced to ancient spring rituals associated with new life and growth.

On this day, some people enjoy dancing around a pole called a maypole, a tradition which originated in fifteenth century England. Participants hold onto ribbon streamers as they dance around the maypole, weaving intricate patterns with the ribbons.

People may also crown a May queen, enjoy a parade, or leave a basket of flowers on a friend's door step!

Maypole

Things you will need

- Maypole pattern (page 39)
- Construction paper
- Several colors of ribbon
- Crayons and markers
- Glue
- Scissors

What to do

1. Color the maypole pattern and cut it out.

2. Glue the maypole pattern to a piece of construction paper.

3. Draw grass, birds, flowers, etc., around the maypole.

4. Glue several ribbons from the top of the maypole to the "ground."

May Day Patterns

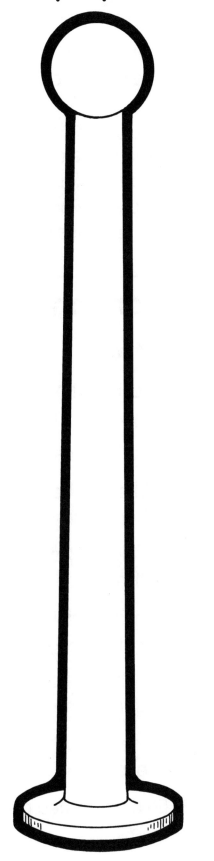
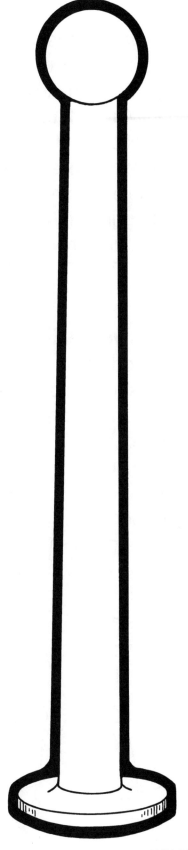

MAY DAY

CINCO DE MAYO

Cinco de Mayo is Spanish for the "fifth of May" and is one of the most important holidays in Mexico. In the United States, it is celebrated in communities where many Mexican-Americans live.

On May 5, 1862, the tiny Mexican army and the large French army fought in the Mexican city of Puebla. By the end of the day, the Mexican army had won a victory which eventually led to the independence of Mexico.

People celebrating Cinco de Mayo enjoy parades, wearing colorful clothing, and feasting on Mexican food. Other festivities include music, dancing, contests, games, and fireworks displays.

Mexican Lantern

Things you will need

- 4 beads
- Construction paper
- Crayons and markers
- Tape
- Hole punch
- Yarn
- Scissors

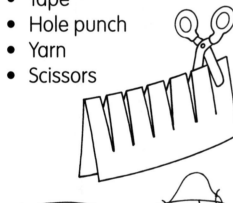

What to do

1. Decorate a piece of construction paper with crayons or markers.

2. Fold the construction paper in half lengthwise.

3. Make cuts beginning at the fold and leaving a 1" border around all edges except on the fold.

4. Unfold the paper and roll it (decorated side out) into a cylinder. Tape the sides together.

5. Punch holes in opposite sides of the lantern's top and string with yarn for hanging.

6. Punch four equally spaced holes around the bottom of the lantern.

7. Place a bead on a piece of yarn and tie a knot under it. Repeat for the other beads.

8. Tie one beaded piece of yarn through each hole.

Mexican Flower

What to do

1. Stack 3-5 different colors and sizes of tissue paper circles on top of each other with the smallest on top.

2. Punch two holes side by side in the center of the stack of tissue paper.

3. Bend the pipe cleaner in half. Then, place each end in a different hole.

4. Make the ends of the pipe cleaner even. Then, twist the ends together to form a stem.

5. Arrange the tissue paper petals as desired.

Things you will need
- Green pipe cleaner
- Tissue paper
- Hole punch
- Scissors

Maraca

Things you will need
- Waxed paper or colored plastic wrap
- Short cardboard tube
- 2 rubber bands
- Dried beans
- Crayons and markers
- Scissors

What to do

1. Decorate a short cardboard tube with markers or crayons.

2. Attach a piece of waxed paper or colored plastic wrap to one end of the tube with a rubber band.

3. Place a handful of dried beans inside the tube.

4. Attach a piece of waxed paper or colored plastic wrap on the other end of the tube with a rubber band.

Sombrero

Things you will need

- Sombrero pattern (below)
- Tan construction paper
- Colorful fabric or ricrac
- Glue
- Markers and crayons
- Gold glitter
- Scissors

What to do

* Teacher: Enlarge the sombrero on tan construction paper.

1. Cut out the sombrero.

2. Decorate the sombrero with markers and crayons.

3. Apply glue in a line across the brim of the hat. Sprinkle gold glitter over the glue. Add colorful fabric or ricrac for decorations.

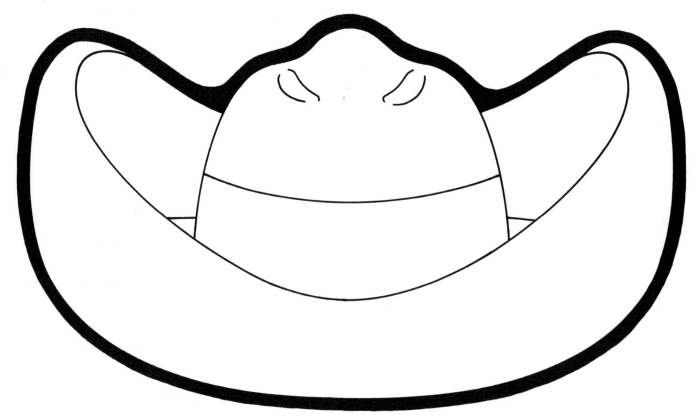

ARBOR DAY

Arbor Day is a special tree planting day held during various times of the year, depending on climate. Arbor Day was first introduced by Julius Sterling Morton in 1872 and celebrated in his home state of Nebraska.

Morton, who was a newspaper publisher, realized the importance of trees to our environment and began a campaign to plant trees across his state. Morton's efforts spread to many other states in the United States and to Canada.

Leaf Prints

Things you will need

- Fresh leaves from different tree species
- Clothespins
- White construction paper
- Scrap paper
- Tempera paint
- Shallow bowls

What to do

1. Gather fresh leaves in a variety of shapes and sizes.

2. Use a clothespin to dip a leaf into a bowl of tempera paint and then place it on a piece of white construction paper.

3. Place a piece of scrap paper on top of the leaf and press the leaf on the construction paper.

4. Continue pressing different leaves into different paint colors and then on the paper.

Fingerprint Tree

Things you will need

- Brown and light blue construction paper
- Green tempera paint
- Crayons
- Glue
- Scissors

What to do

1. Cut out a tree trunk shape from brown construction paper.

2. Glue the tree trunk to a piece of light blue construction paper.

3. Dip your thumb or finger in green paint and make fingerprint leaves for the tree.

4. Draw a sun, birds, and clouds in the sky and grass on the ground.

Apple Tree

What to do

1. Cut out a tree trunk shape from brown construction paper.

2. Glue the tree trunk to a piece of white construction paper.

3. Crumple up green tissue paper and glue it above the trunk to make leaves.

4. Crumple up a few pieces of red tissue paper and place the pieces among the green tissue paper for apples.

Things you will need

- Brown and white construction paper
- Green and red tissue paper
- Glue
- Scissors

MOTHER'S DAY

Mother's Day, the second Sunday in May, is a day set apart for honoring all mothers.

Julia Ward Howard first made a suggestion for Mother's Day as early as 1872 as a day dedicated to peace. In 1875, Anna Jarvis began a nationwide campaign for a day to honor mothers. President Woodrow Wilson proclaimed Mother's Day as a national observance in 1915.

Celebrations of Mother's Day include visits, cards, gifts, and special dinners.

My Hands

Things you will need
- Lace or ribbon
- Construction paper
- Yarn or ribbon
- Glue
- Crayons or markers
- Hole punch

What to do

1. On a piece of construction paper, trace around both hands.

2. Cut out and color the hand shapes.

3. Glue the hand shapes to a piece of construction paper.

4. Write a Mother's Day message on the paper.

5. Punch one hole at each side of the paper's top. String yarn or ribbon through the holes and tie a knot.

6. Glue lace or ribbon around the back edge of the paper and allow the glue to dry.

Plant a Flower for Mom

Things you will need

- Buttons, sequins, glitter, ricrac, etc.
- Live potted flower
- Potting soil
- Water
- Brightly-colored plastic cup
- Markers
- Glue

What to do

* Teacher: Write the child's name on the bottom of the cup.

1. Decorate the cup with buttons, sequins, glitter, ricrac, etc.

2. Fill the cup $2/3$ full with soil.

3. Plant a flower in the cup and water the flower.

Flower Garden for Mom

Things you will need

- Flower and leaf patterns (page 48)
- Construction paper
- Glue stick
- Markers
- Scissors

What to do

* Teacher: Copy four flowers and eight leaves on colored construction paper.

1. Cut out the flowers and leaves.

2. Cut "grass" from long rectangles of green construction paper cut halfway down, as shown. Cut stems from thin strips of green construction paper.

3. Glue the pieces to the construction paper in the following order: flowers, stems, leaves, and grass.

4. Write "Happy Mother's Day" on the garden picture.

Flower on a Stick Card

Things you will need

- Flower pattern (bottom of page 48)
- Construction paper
- Glue
- Pencil
- Crayons or markers
- Craft stick
- Scissors

What to do

* Teacher: Copy the flower card pattern on a piece of construction paper.

1. Fold the construction paper along the straight edge of the flower.

2. Color the flower.

3. Cut out the flower shape, being careful not to cut the fold of the flower petal (as shown).

4. Open the card and write a message inside.

5. Color a craft stick green and glue it to the back of the card.

Mother's Day Patterns

MOTHER'S DAY

FLAG DAY

The people of the United States observe Flag Day on June 14. On that day in 1777, leaders of the American colonies voted to accept a new flag as the national symbol. In 1877, Flag Day was first officially observed when Congress declared that the flag should be flown over public buildings to celebrate the 100th anniversary of the flag as a national symbol. June 14 has been officially recognized as Flag Day since 1949 when President Harry Truman signed the National Flag Day Bill.

Originally, the United States flag had 13 stripes and 13 stars. The flag changed as more states joined the Union. The flag Americans use today was designed when Hawaii became the fiftieth state in 1960. Each of the fifty stars represents a state and the thirteen stripes represent the thirteen original colonies.

Yarn Flag

Things you will need

- White tagboard
- Unsharpened pencil
- Blue marker
- White or silver star stickers
- Glue
- 4 pieces of thick, red yarn, 5½" long
- 3 pieces of thick, red yarn, 3" long
- Scissors
- Ruler

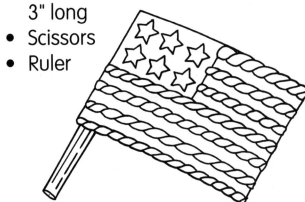

What to do

* Teacher: Before beginning this activity, talk about the flag's changes since 1777.

1. Outline a 2" x 2½" rectangle in the upper left corner of a piece of 4½" x 5½" tagboard.

2. Color the rectangle blue and place rows of star stickers on the rectangle.

3. Glue yarn to the tagboard for the flag's stripes. Start by gluing a 3" piece of red yarn to the top. Then, leave a white space. Continue until all yarn is glued to tagboard.

4. Tape a pencil on the back of the flag for the flag pole.

Wind Sock

Things you will need

- Blue poster board, 18" x 18"
- 2 each of red, white, and blue streamers, 30" long
- Star stickers
- White construction paper
- Glue stick
- Clear tape
- Scissors
- Hole punch
- Red yarn, 14" long

What to do

1. Place the blue poster board flat on a table.

2. Decorate the poster board with star stickers or star shapes cut from white construction paper.

3. Roll the poster board into a cylinder shape. Overlap the edges about 1" and tape the sides together.

4. Punch 4 evenly-spaced holes around the top of the cylinder. In each hole, tie a 14" piece of red yarn, bring the four pieces of yarn together and tie them into a knot.

5. Cut two 30" long streamers of each color: red, white, and blue.

6. Tape the streamers to the inside of the bottom of the cylinder.

FATHER'S DAY

Father's Day, which is observed on the third Sunday in June, has been celebrated since 1910.

The idea for this day started in 1909 with Sonora Louise Smart Dodd of Spokane, Washington. She thought that fathers, like mothers, should be honored with a special day. Several efforts were made to make Father's Day a national holiday, but only in 1972 did President Richard Nixon sign the observance into law.

Many people celebrate this day with visits, special dinners, cards, and gifts.

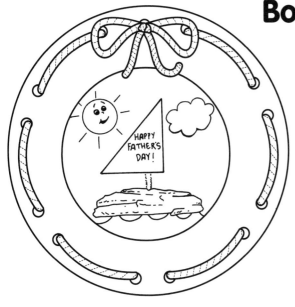

Boat Picture

What to do

1. Cut a circle from a piece of light blue construction paper. Then, punch evenly-spaced holes around the edge.

2. Draw in a second circle and a water line, as shown.

3. Glue a piece of tree bark on the water line for the base of a boat. Glue a pretzel stick above the bark for the mast.

4. Cut a white paper triangle for a sail. Write "Happy Father's Day" on the triangle. Glue the sail above the pretzel.

5. Cut a yellow circle and a white cloud and glue to the inside circle, as shown.

6. To finish the picture, "sew" around the edge through the punched holes with twine and tie a bow at the top.

Things you will need
- Light blue, white, and yellow construction paper
- Tree bark
- Pretzel stick
- Twine
- Glue
- Hole punch
- Crayons or markers
- Scissors

Rock Animal

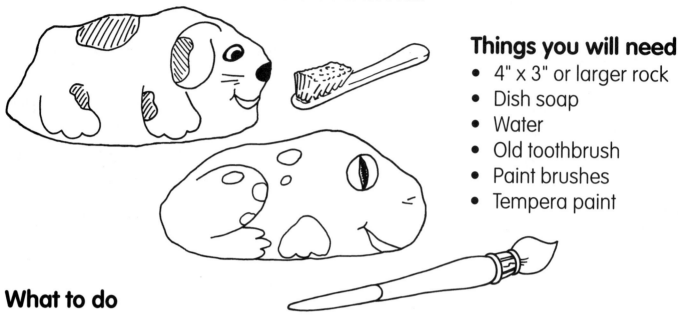

Things you will need
- 4" x 3" or larger rock
- Dish soap
- Water
- Old toothbrush
- Paint brushes
- Tempera paint

What to do

1. Scrub the rock with soapy water and an old toothbrush. Allow the rock dry.

2. Paint the rock to look like your father's favorite animal.

Truck Picture

Things you will need
- Truck pattern (page 53)
- Construction paper
- Aluminum foil
- Glue
- Markers
- Scissors

What to do

1. Color and cut out the truck pattern.

2. Glue the truck pattern to a piece of construction paper.

3. Cut out two small circles from aluminum foil for hubcaps and glue to the truck.

4. Write a Father's Day message around the truck.

Father's Day Pattern

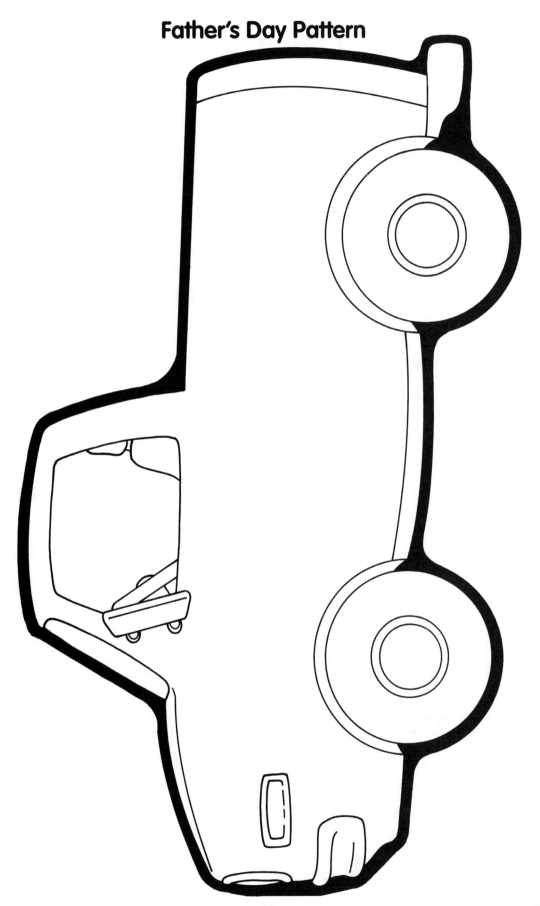

53

FOURTH OF JULY

On July 4, 1776, in Philadelphia, Pennsylvania, the Continental Congress adopted the Declaration of Independence. The Declaration, which explained the grievances of the American colonies against the British king, George, was drafted by Thomas Jefferson. The ringing of the Liberty Bell announced the signing of the Declaration of Independence.

Fourth of July, or Independence Day, celebrations include gatherings of family and friends, festivals, picnics, outdoor concerts, and fireworks displays.

Happy Birthday U.S.A.

Things you will need

- Cupcake top and candle patterns (page 56)
- Light-blue or white construction paper
- Cupcake paper
- Sprinkles, colored sugar, or confetti
- Glue
- Red and blue crayons and markers
- Scissors

What to do

1. Cut out and color the cupcake top and candle patterns.

2. Draw red stripes on a piece of light blue or white construction paper.

3. Glue the cupcake top and candle to the middle of the construction paper.

4. Cut a cupcake paper in fourths and glue a section underneath the cupcake top.

5. Glue sprinkles, confetti, or colored sugar to the cupcake top.

6. Write an Independence Day message on the construction paper around the completed cupcake.

Firecracker Roll-Up

Things you will need
- White bread
- Blueberry jelly
- Red licorice
- Knife
- Craft stick

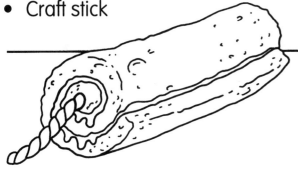

What to do

* Teacher: Before beginning, cut the crust off of a piece of white bread.

1. Use a craft stick to spread blueberry jelly on the bread.

2. Place a piece of red licorice in the center of the bread with one end extended out of the bread.

3. Roll the bread up with the licorice in the center to look like a firecracker.

4. Enjoy the "firecracker" as a snack.

Liberty Bell

Things you will need
- Liberty Bell pattern (page 56)
- Gray construction paper
- Small twig
- 8" piece of yarn
- Hole punch
- Scissors

What to do

* Teacher: Copy the Liberty Bell pattern on gray construction paper.

1. Cut out the Liberty Bell pattern.

2. Punch a hole in the top of the Liberty Bell.

3. Loop a piece of yarn through the hole and tie the bell pattern tightly to a twig.

Fourth of July Patterns

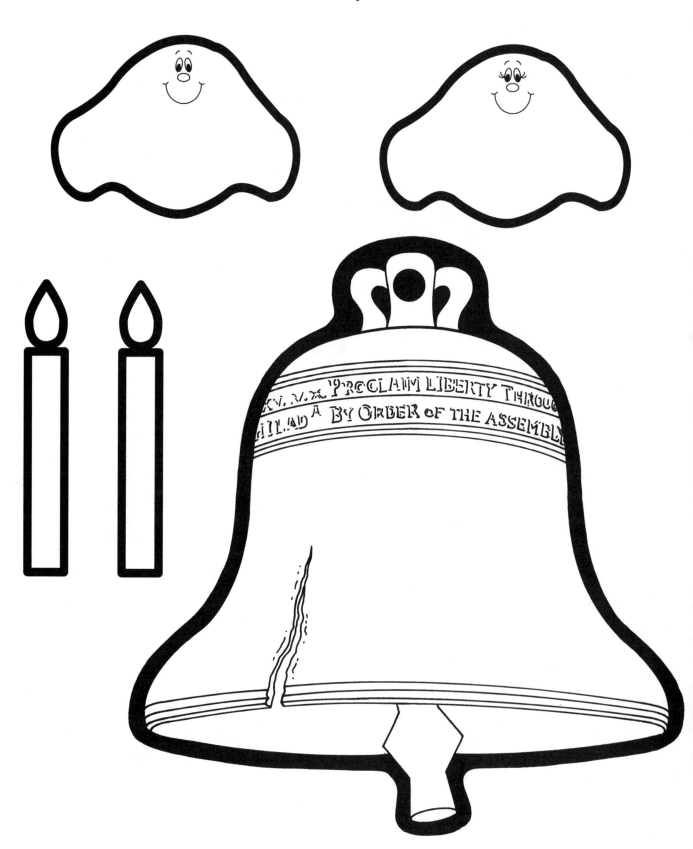

ROSH HASHANAH

Rosh Hashanah, which means "beginning of the year" in Hebrew, is the Jewish New Year. Usually falling in September, Rosh Hashanah is observed for one or two days.

Rosh Hashanah is both a joyful and serious time. It is a time for self-examination, remembrance, and blowing the shofar.

The shofar is a wind instrument made from a ram's horn which is blown in the temple to mark the beginning of the High Holy Days.

On the first day of Rosh Hashanah, Jews visit a body of flowing water (which may or may not contain fish). The fish, who depend on water, symbolize Jewish people, who depend on God. On this day, Jews also eat apple slices, ball-shaped challah bread dipped in honey, and other foods sweetened with honey, hoping the year will be full of blessings.

Fish

Things you will need

- Wiggly eyes
- 2" x 11" strip of light blue construction paper
- Tape
- Crayons and markers
- Scissors

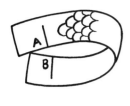
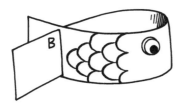

What to do

1. Cut a 2" x 11" strip from light blue construction paper.

2. Cut a 1" slit 1" from each end of the strip. One slit should begin from the bottom side of the strip and the other should begin from the top (see diagram).

3. Decorate the strip to look like a fish.

4. Place the end slit A inside the end of slit B so that the strip forms a fish shape (see diagram).

5. Tape the overlapping strips in place.

6. Glue on wiggly eyes.

Shofar

Things you will need

- Shofar pattern (below)
- Brown construction paper
- Tagboard
- Brown yarn or twine
- Glue
- Scissors

What to do

* Teacher: Copy the shofar on brown construction paper.

1. Cut out the shofar pattern.

2. Glue the shofar to tagboard and cut out.

3. Cover the circular end of the shofar with glue.

4. Starting along the outer edge, glue the yarn or twine in a spiral to cover the end.

5. Cover the remaining part of the shofar with glue.

6. Cover the rest of the shofar with yarn or twine as shown.

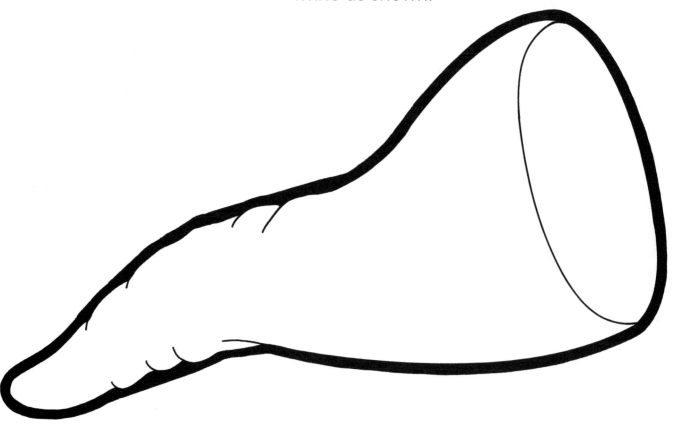

Apple Slice Magnet

Things you will need
- Apple slice patterns (below)
- Sharp knife
- Red and white construction paper
- 1 apple seed
- Glue
- Self-adhesive magnet
- Scissors
- Apples
- Honey (optional)

What to do

* Teacher: Before the activity, slice apples and show the class a real apple slice. Then, remove the apple seeds for use in the craft.

* Copy the large slice pattern on red paper and the small slice pattern on white paper.

1. Cut out the apple slice shapes.

2. Glue the white shape inside the red shape.

3. Glue a real apple seed to the white construction paper.

4. Attach a self-adhesive magnet to the back of the apple slice.

* After completing the craft, enjoy real apples dipped in honey as a snack.

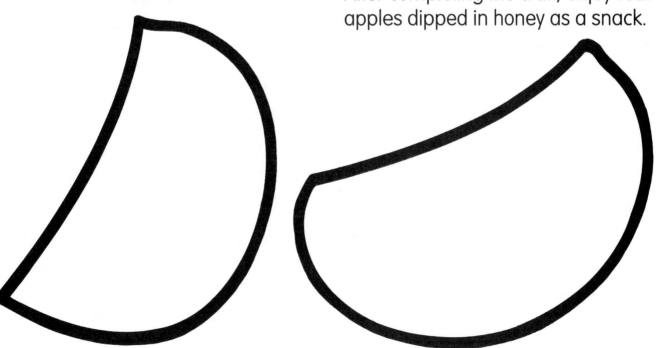

YOM KIPPUR

Yom Kippur, the Day of Atonement, is the most sacred Jewish holiday and is known as the Sabbath of the Sabbaths. It is a special day when people dress in special clothing and the synagogue is decorated. On Yom Kippur, Jews look forward to a fresh start for the new year.

Yom Kippur is a ritual-filled day for prayer, self-reflection, confession, repentance, reading from the Torah, and fasting. Through fasting, Jews are able to concentrate more fully on the holiday. At the end of the fast, Jewish families come together for a special meal.

Yom Kippur ends with the blowing of the shofar at the synagogue .

Self-Reflection

Things you will need
- Wallpaper and cloth scraps, buttons, etc.
- Construction paper
- Crayons and markers
- Old magazines
- Scissors
- Yarn
- Glue

What to do

1. Cut out magazine pictures of things which show kindness and caring for others, such as helping around the house, taking care of an animal, drawing a picture for a sick relative, etc.

2. Glue the magazine pictures around the edge of a piece of construction paper to make a frame.

3. Fill in gaps between pictures by writing words like "kindness, caring, helping, thoughtful, loving," etc.

4. Draw a self-portrait in the center of the frame. Add yarn hair, clothes made from wallpaper and cloth scraps, and real buttons.

Jonah and the Whale

Things you will need
- Whale and Jonah patterns (page 62)
- Tagboard
- Blue plastic wrap
- Crayons and markers
- Glue
- Clear tape
- Scissors

What to do

* Enlarge the patterns onto white construction paper.

* Teacher: Before beginning this activity, tell the class the story of Jonah and the Whale.

> One day, God told a man named Jonah to go to the city of Ninevah. God told Jonah to tell the people there to stop the bad things they were doing. Jonah did not do as God said. Instead, he got on a ship and tried to sail away from God. God sent a big storm to follow Jonah. The sailors on the ship asked Jonah why the storm had come. Jonah said that God had sent the storm to follow him. Jonah told the sailors that if they threw him into the ocean, the storm would stop. The sailors threw Jonah into the ocean, the storm stopped, and Jonah was swallowed by a whale. For three days and nights, Jonah lived inside the whale, and asked God to save him. The whale spit Jonah out and Jonah went to Ninevah where he told the people to stop doing bad things. The people of Ninevah listened to Jonah and started doing good things instead.

1. Color and cut out the patterns.

2. Make a frame from tagboard by cutting two 1" x 11" strips and two 1" x 8" strips and gluing them together in a rectangle.

3. Stretch a piece of blue plastic wrap tightly over the frame and tape it to the back of all four sides of the frame.

4. Tape the whale and Jonah patterns to the underside of the plastic wrap so they appear to be swimming in the water.

Yom Kippur Patterns

HALLOWEEN

Halloween is celebrated on October 31, a day on which many children dress up in costumes and go door-to-door trick-or-treating. People also attend carnivals, parties, and haunted houses.

Halloween customs were started by the Celts, an ancient people who lived in northern France and the British Isles, to celebrate their New Year's Eve which fell on October 31—the beginning of winter. On that night, the Celts believed evil spirits roamed the earth, so they built bonfires to scare the spirits away.

The trick-or-treat custom started in Ireland when people went from house to house to beg for food. Those who gave food were wished good luck for the next year—those who did not give food were wished bad luck.

Ireland is the only country where Halloween is a national holiday.

Ghost Prints

Things you will need
- Black construction paper
- White tempera paint
- Black marker
- Small star stickers
- Bare feet

What to do

1. Have each child step in white tempera paint (in bare feet) and then onto the center of a piece of black construction paper.

2. Wash and dry each student's feet.

3. After the paint dries, turn the papers so the prints are upside down. Use the black marker to add faces on the "ghosts" and stick star stickers in the night sky.

Mini Witch's Hat

Things you will need

- Hat patterns (page 67)
- Black construction paper
- White crayon
- Glue
- Tape
- Scissors

What to do

1. Cut out the hat patterns. Trace the patterns onto black construction paper with a white crayon and cut out.

2. According to the diagram, bend point A and point B around to form a cone and tape it closed.

3. Glue the cone to the circle and let it dry.

Finger Puppets

Things you will need

- Halloween patterns (page 68)
- Construction paper
- Crayons and markers
- Glue stick
- Scissors

What to do

1. Cut out the patterns.

2. Color the patterns as desired.

3. Place glue around the edges of matching shapes and place the shapes back-to-back, making sure to leave space in the middle to fit a finger.

Candy Corn Napkin Rings

Things you will need
- Cardboard tubes
- Candy corn
- Tempera paint
- Paintbrushes
- Glue
- Scissors

What to do

* Teacher: Cut a cardboard tube into 1" sections and give each child a section.

1. Paint the section orange, yellow, or white.

2. Glue candy corn around the cardboard tube section.

Door Ghost

Things you will need
- Ghost pattern (page 68)
- Tagboard
- Black yarn
- Hole punch
- Black markers
- Glue
- Scissors

What to do

* Teacher: Enlarge the ghost pattern.

1. Cut out the ghost pattern and glue the pattern to tagboard.

2. Cut out the tagboard shape and punch a hole in the top.

3. Loop a piece of yarn through the hole for hanging.

4. Hang the ghost on a door for decoration.

Jack-o'-Lantern Face

Things you will need

- Jack-o'-lantern face pattern (page 69)
- Orange construction paper
- Poster board
- Yellow tempera paint
- Paintbrush
- Yellow yarn
- Pencils
- Scissors

What to do

* Teacher: Before beginning this activity, cut out the jack-o'-lantern face and make a template from poster board.

1. Cut out a pumpkin shape from orange construction paper. (As an option, use an enlarged pumpkin pattern from page 68 as a guide.)

2. Trace the jack-o'-lantern face on the pumpkin shape.

3. Paint the jack-o'-lantern face yellow.

4. Punch a hole in the top of the pumpkin and string with yellow yarn for hanging.

Halloween Patterns

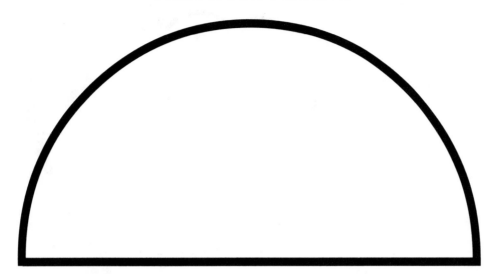

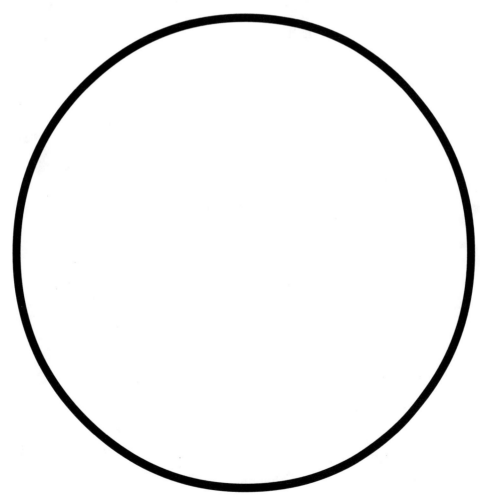

Halloween Patterns

Halloween Patterns

ELECTION DAY

Election Day is held on the Tuesday after the first Monday in November. It is a day set aside for the American people to select officials who will run the federal, state and city governments. People may also vote on amendments to the United States Constitution, laws, and tax levies. Every four years, United States citizens vote for a new president and vice president.

All citizens eighteen years of age and older can register to vote, but there are certain restrictions. Voters must be U.S. citizens, must not have committed a serious crime, must be of sound mind, and must have lived in their community for a certain period of time.

Voting is done by a secret ballot, to ensure privacy. Polling places are held in public buildings such as schools, churches, and fire stations.

Election Day Ballot Box

Things you will need
- Ballot pattern (page 71)
- Large sheets of white paper
- Cardboard box
- Crayons and markers
- Pencils
- Glue and tape
- Scissors or craft knife

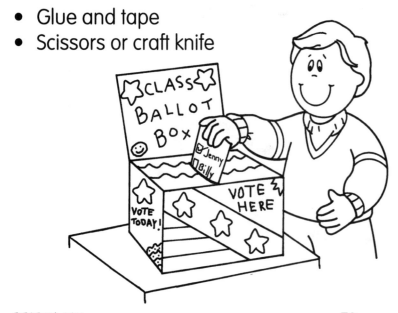

What to do

* Teacher: Make a class ballot box by covering a cardboard box with white paper and cutting a slit in the top.

1. Let each student draw an election-day-related picture, symbol, or phrase on the box.

2. As a class, decide on an issue or item about which to vote, such as class mascot, class officers, etc.

3. Use the ballot patterns on page 71 to hold a class election.

Election Day Patterns

VETERANS DAY

Veterans Day, formerly known as Armistice Day, was signed into law on June 1, 1954 by President Eisenhower. November 11 is a day to honor and remember all those who have served in the Armed Forces of the United States and veterans of all wars.

Each Veterans Day at Arlington National Cemetery, in Virginia, a ceremony is held in which a wreath is laid on the Tomb of the Unknowns where four unknown servicemen are buried.

Veterans Day is celebrated with ceremonies, wreath layings, and parades.

Bowl Helmets

Things you will need
- White paper bowls
- Star stickers
- Markers or crayons
- Hole punch
- Yarn
- Glue

What to do
1. Decorate the outside of a paper bowl with crayons, markers, star stickers, etc., to look like a helmet.
2. Punch holes on opposite sides of the bowl and tie a piece of yarn through each hole. Tie the ends together to make a chin strap.

Veterans Day Plane

Things you will need
- Plane patterns (page 74)
- Blue and white construction paper
- Hole punch
- String
- Crayons and markers
- Clear tape
- Scissors

What to do

* Teacher: Copy the plane patterns on blue construction paper.

1. Cut out the plane patterns.

2. Decorate the two pieces of the plane with markers and crayons.

3. Cut a slit on the dotted line of the body pattern and slide the wings through the slit.

4. Tape the wings securely to the plane body.

5. Punch a hole at the top of the plane body and loop a piece of string through the hole.

6. Hang the plane from the ceiling or "fly" the plane around the room.

Veterans Day Patterns

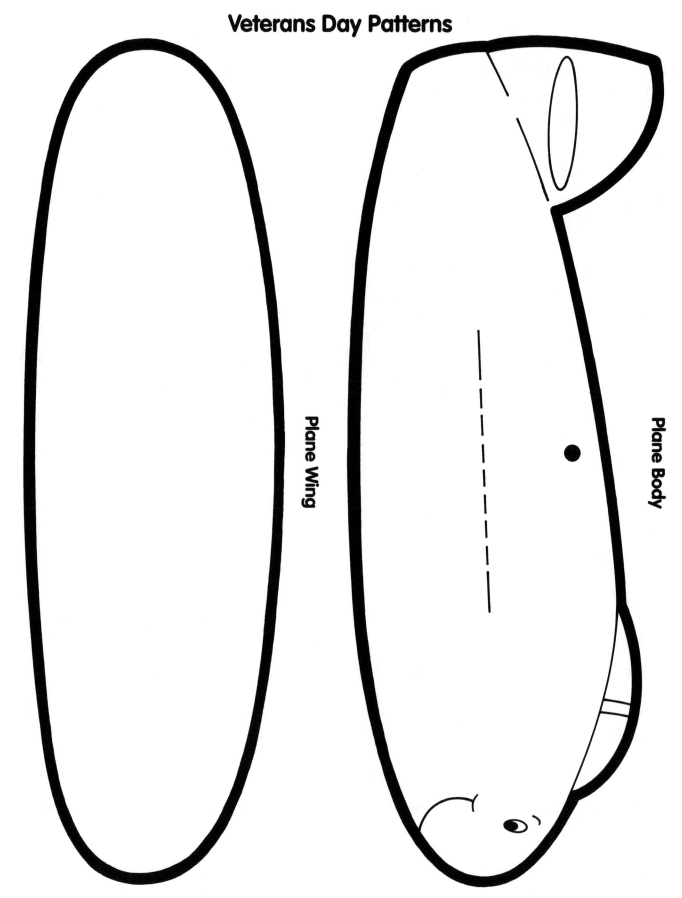

Plane Wing

Plane Body

THANKSGIVING

Thanksgiving is observed in the United States on the fourth Thursday in November and in Canada on the second Monday in October.

In the United States, the first Thanksgiving was celebrated at Plymouth, Massachusetts in 1621, one year after the Pilgrims landed at Plymouth Rock. During their first year in their new home, many Pilgrims died because they did not have enough food. The Native Americans were kind to the Pilgrims and showed them how to hunt, fish, and how to grow corn and other vegetables.

When the Pilgrims and Native Americans had the first Thanksgiving feast, they gave thanks for their food and their health and safety.

Today, people in both the United States and Canada celebrate Thanksgiving with family and friends and a large meal. A Thanksgiving feast might include: turkey, stuffing, vegetables, sweet potatoes, cranberries, and pumpkin pie.

My Thankful Book

Things you will need

- Pilgrim Bear pattern (page 79)
- Fall-colored construction paper
- Old magazines
- Markers or crayons
- Hole punch
- Yarn
- Glue

What to do

* Teacher: Enlarge the Pilgrim Bear onto white construction paper.

1. Hold 3 pieces of construction paper together.

2. Punch 2 holes near the edge and tie the construction paper together with yarn.

3. Color the Pilgrim Bear, cut it out, and glue it on the front of the booklet. Write the words "My Thankful Book" over the bear.

4. Cut or tear out magazine pictures of things for which you are thankful. Draw in other pictures.

5. Glue the pictures on the pages to complete the "My Thankful Book."

Jack

Horn of Plenty

What to do

* Teacher: Copy the fruit, vegetable, and nut patterns onto colored construction paper.

1. Cut out the patterns.

2. Cut a cornucopia shape from gold paper. Glue the shape to construction paper.

3. Glue the fruits, vegetables, and nuts to the "open" end of the cornucopia.

Things you will need

- Fruit, vegetable, and nut patterns (page 80)
- Colored construction paper
- Scissors
- Glue

Mr. Turkey

Things you will need

- Turkey feather and head patterns (page 79)
- Fall-colored construction paper
- Scrap paper or newspaper
- Brown paper lunch sack
- Crayons or markers
- Glue
- Stapler and staples
- Scissors

What to do

* Teacher: Copy eight feathers on colored paper. Copy the head on red paper.

1. Cut out the feather and head patterns.

2. Fill a paper lunch sack with scrap paper or newspaper.

3. Fold the front of the sack flat and staple it closed.

4. Glue the face to the top of the sack front and the feathers to the sack back.

The Mayflower

Things you will need

- White foam cup
- White construction paper
- Plastic straw
- Craft clay
- Hole punch
- Scissors

What to do

* Teacher: Cut $^2/_3$ off the top of a foam cup.

1. Place a lump of craft clay in the bottom of the cup.

2. Make a paper sail by cutting a square from construction paper. Punch two holes in a line at the top and bottom of the square.

3. Cut a straw in half and place the straw through the holes in the sail.

4. Attach the bottom of the straw to the lump of clay in the cup bottom.

Harvest Corn

Things you will need

- Short cardboard tube
- Colored popcorn kernels or aquarium rocks
- Raffia
- Glue

What to do

1. Cover a short cardboard tube with glue.

2. Roll the cardboard tube in colored popcorn until covered.

3. Allow the glue to dry.

4. Glue raffia to one end of the tube to look like corn silks.

Pilgrim Mural

Things you will need

- Hat and bonnet patterns (page 81)
- Large roll of white butcher paper
- Aluminum foil
- Buttons
- Pencils
- Crayons and markers
- Scissors

What to do

* Teacher: Before beginning this activity, show the class pictures of people dressed in colonial clothing.

* Cut sections of butcher paper on which two students can lie down.

* If desired, enlarge the hat or bonnet patterns for students.

1. Color and cut out the hat or bonnet pattern.

2. Allow pairs of students to trace each other's body shapes on the paper.

3. Draw pilgrim-type clothes on each figure. Use aluminum foil for buckles and real buttons on clothes.

4. Tape the completed drawings on the wall as a mural.

5. Allow each student to take home his drawing after the display is complete.

Thanksgiving Patterns

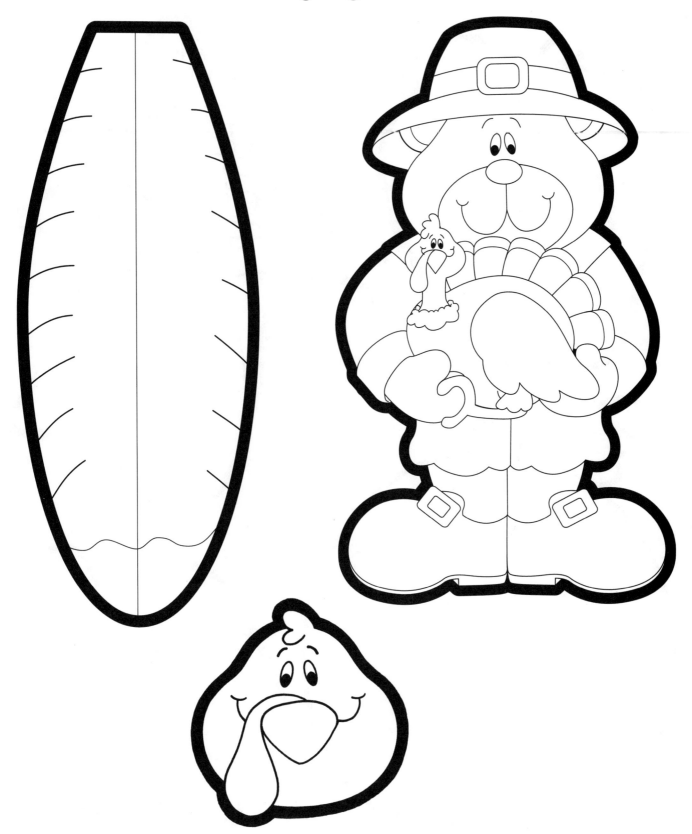

Thanksgiving Patterns

Thanksgiving Patterns

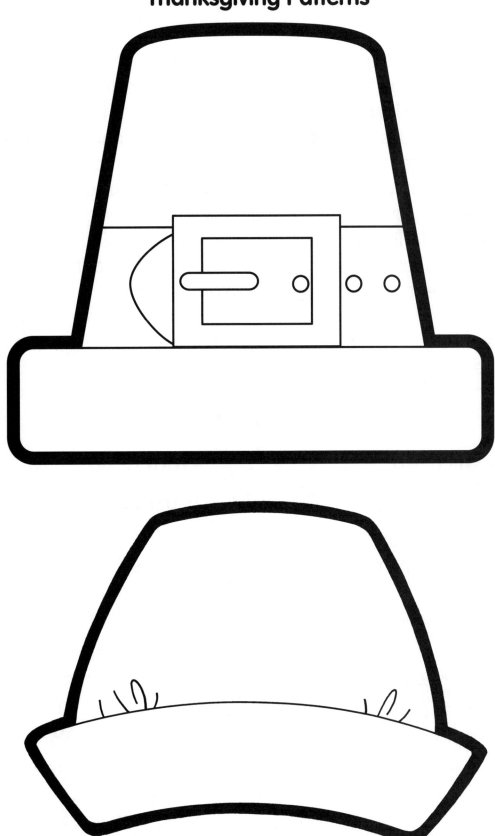

HANUKKAH

Hanukkah is an annual eight-day Jewish celebration. Hanukkah usually comes in the month of December and is also known as the "Festival of Lights."

In the year 165 BC (Jews use the term BCE, or Before the Common Era) the Assyrian-Greeks took over the Temple in Jerusalem. A small army of Jews led by Judah Maccabee defeated the Assyrian-Greeks. After reclaiming the Temple, the group could find only a small amount of holy oil which could be used to light the temple menorah, but that oil miraculously burned for eight days. Because the oil burned for eight days, the menorah has eight candles plus one extra candle to light the others. On each day of Hanukkah, an additional candle is lit.

Many Jewish people celebrate Hanukkah by lighting the candles of the Menorah. The special Menorah used for Hanukkah is called the Hanukkiah. During these special eight days, people enjoy storytelling, gift-giving, special holiday foods, and the dreidel game.

Hanukkiah

Things you will need
- Dark-colored construction paper
- Orange tissue paper
- Kitchen sponges cut in half
- Yellow tempera paint mixed with gold glitter
- White tempera paint
- Glue

What to do
1. Dip a sponge in the glitter and paint mixture.

2. Press the sponge onto paper to form a Menorah shape (see diagram).

3. Dip another sponge in white paint and make 4 short candles on each side of a taller center candle.

4. Crumple up orange tissue paper and glue it to the top of each candle for a flame.

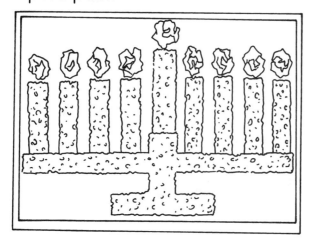

Dough Dreidel

Things you will need

- Dreidel or dreidel pictures
- Waxed paper
- Tempera paint or markers
- Paintbrushes
- Glue
- Plastic straw, cut in half

- Play Dough:
  - 4 tsp. corn starch
  - 4½ cups flour
  - 1 cup salt
  - 2 tbs. vegetable oil
  - 2 cups water

- 4 drops vanilla or peppermint extract
- Mixing bowl
- Mixing spoon

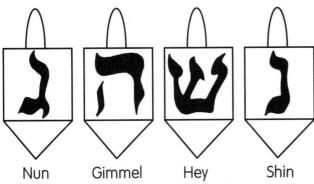

Nun   Gimmel   Hey   Shin

When the first letters of each of the Hebrew words (Nun, Gimmel, Hey, and Shin) are put together, they mean "A great miracle happened here."

What to do

* Show the class dreidel pictures or real dreidels.

1. Make play dough with the children by combining the recipe ingredients above. The recipe will make about twenty-four ¼ cup dreidels. Note: Tell the children that the dough is not edible.

2. Mold ¼ cup of dough into the shape of a dreidel (see diagram). Mold a handle from dough or push a straw into the dreidel top.

3. Allow the dough to dry for 1-2 days. Turn the dreidel often to make sure dough dries completely.

4. After the dreidel dries, draw, paint, or glue a different dreidel letter (copied from above) onto each side of the dreidel.

CHRISTMAS

Christmas is celebrated by Christians on December 25, as the birthday of Jesus Christ.

No one knows exactly when Jesus was born, but about the year 350, a church in Rome decided that Christ's Mass, a church service marking the birth of Jesus, should be held on December 25. "Christ's Mass" eventually became Christmas.

Santa Claus, a legendary man who delivers gifts to children across the world, is based on Saint Nicholas and became a popular figure in the 1800's. The name Santa Claus came about when Dutch settlers to the U.S. called Saint Nicholas by his Dutch name, "Sinterklaas," and the word sounded like "Santa Claus."

Many families have their own Christmas traditions which include decorating Christmas trees, singing carols, attending church, and giving gifts.

Tree Centerpiece

Things you will need

- Triangle tree pattern (page 89)
- Green construction paper
- Colored ring cereal
- Glitter, sequins, etc.
- Star stickers
- Clear tape
- Glue
- Scissors

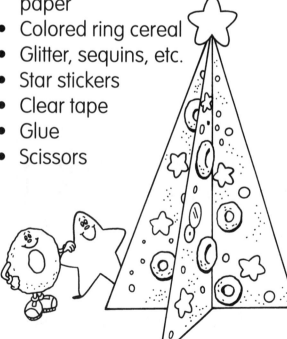

What to do

* Teacher: Make two copies of the triangle tree pattern on green construction paper.

1. Cut out the two triangles.

2. Fold the two triangles in half lengthwise.

3. Place the folded triangles back-to-back and tape them together with clear tape.

4. Stand the four-sided tree upright.

5. Glue colored ring cereal, glitter, sequins, etc., to the tree.

6. Place two star stickers back-to-back on the top of the tree.

Candy Cane Ornament

Things you will need

- Candy cane pattern (page 89)
- White tagboard
- 1" red and white pom poms
- Glue
- Hole punch
- Red ribbon
- Scissors

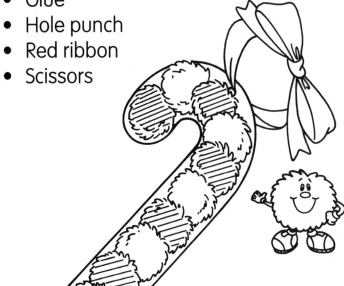

What to do

* Teacher: Copy the candy cane pattern on tagboard.

1. Cut out the candy cane and punch a hole in the top.

2. Cover the shape with glue, being careful not to cover the hole.

3. Cover the pattern with alternating "stripes" of red and white pom poms, following the pattern.

4. Punch a hole in the top of the candy cane.

5. Tie on a red ribbon through the hole for a hanger.

Pasta Tree

Things you will need

- Tagboard
- Pasta shapes
- Sequins, glitter, ricrac, etc.
- Scissors

What to do

1. Cut out a tree shape from tagboard.

2. Glue on pasta shapes, glitter, sequins, ricrac, etc. for decorations.

   CHRISTMAS

Santa with Bag

Things you need

- Santa head and bag patterns (page 90)
- Cotton balls
- 2 tongue depressors or craft sticks
- Aluminum foil
- Glue
- Markers
- Scissors

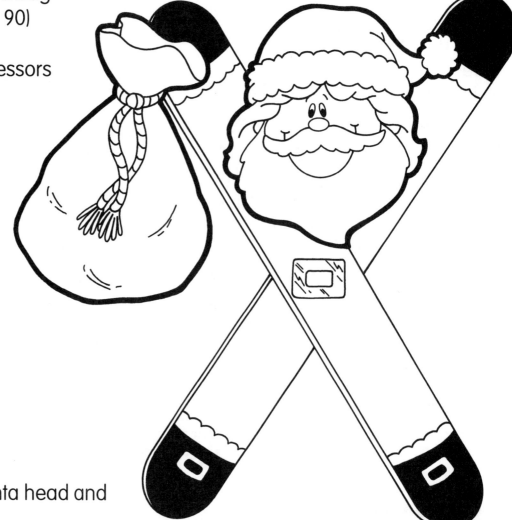

What to do

1. Cut out the Santa head and bag patterns.

2. Color two tongue depressors red with black tips for boots and mittens.

3. Glue the two tongue depressors together to form an X and allow to dry.

4. Make a buckle from aluminum foil and glue it to the middle of the X.

5. Glue the bag to one of Santa's hands.

6. Glue on Santa's head.

7. Glue on stretched cotton for Santa's hair, beard, hatband, and the tip of his hat.

Stocking

Things you will need

- Stocking patterns (page 91)
- Construction paper
- Yarn
- Hole punch
- Crayon and markers
- Scissors

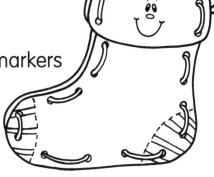

What to do

* Teacher: Enlarge the two stocking patterns on construction paper.

1. Color and cut out the patterns.

2. Punch holes in both stockings according to the circles.

3. Sew the stocking copies together with yarn.

Snowman Ornament

Things you will need

- Snowman pattern (page 90)
- White construction paper
- White yarn
- Paintbrushes
- Hole punch
- Scissors

- Sparkly paint
  - 4 tsp. salt
  - 2 tsp. liquid starch
  - 5 drops white liquid tempera paint
  - Mixing bowl
  - Mixing spoon

What to do

* Teacher: Copy the snowman on white construction paper.

* Mix together the ingredients for sparkly paint. Double the recipe as needed.

1. Cut out the snowman pattern.

2. Paint the snowman with sparkly paint and allow to dry.

3. Punch a hole in the top of the snowman and tie white yarn through the hole for a hanger.

Rudolph

Things you will need

- Heart-shaped Rudolph head pattern (page 90)
- Black, red, and brown construction paper
- Wiggly eyes
- Pencils
- Glue
- Scissors

What to do

* Enlarge the heart-shaped head pattern on brown construction paper.

1. Trace both hands onto black construction paper and cut them out.

2. Cut out the Rudolph head pattern.

3. Glue each hand to the back of the head pattern (see diagram).

4. Cut out a circle from red construction paper for Rudolph's nose.

5. Glue on wiggly eyes and the red nose.

Ho! Ho!

Things you will need

- Red and white construction paper
- Cotton balls
- Crayons or markers
- Glue
- Scissors

What to do

1. Cut out a red oval shape for Santa's head (about 6" x 7").

2. Draw in Santa's face with crayons or markers.

3. Cut out five to eight white construction paper strips and glue to Santa's chin for a beard.

4. Glue on cotton balls for hair, eyebrows, and a mustache.

Christmas Patterns

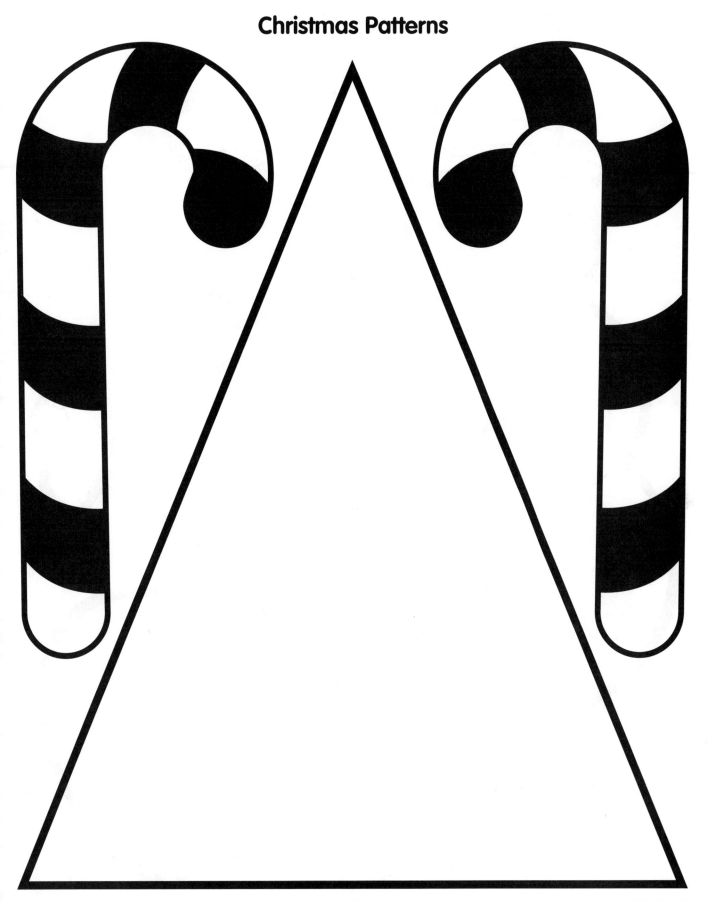

CHRISTMAS

Christmas Patterns

Christmas Patterns

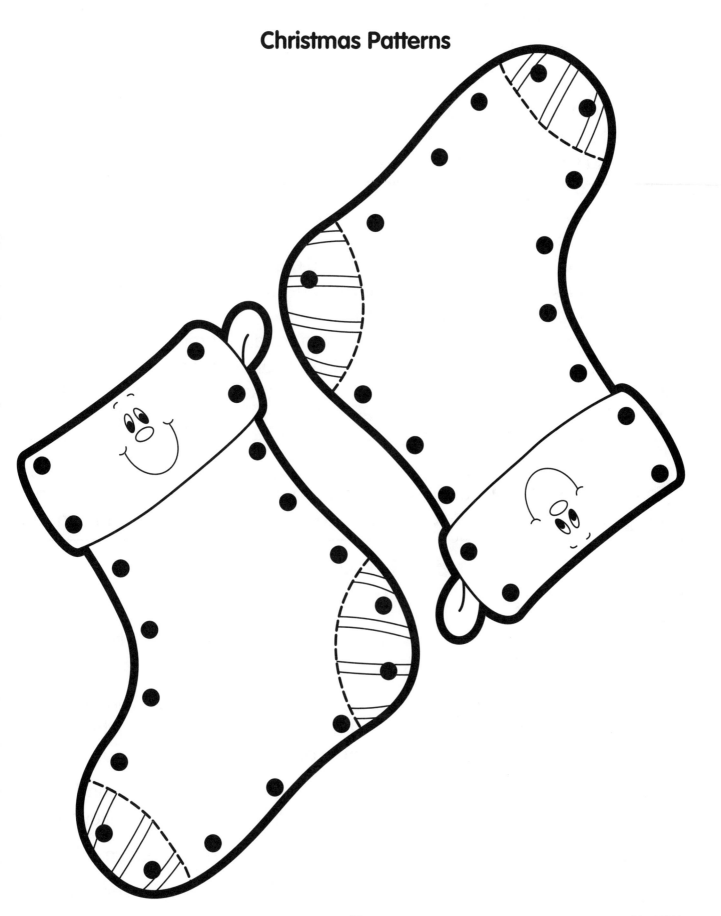

KWANZAA

Kwanzaa, a holiday celebrated by African Americans, begins on December 26 and lasts for seven days, until January 1.

Kwanzaa was started in the United States in 1966 by Dr. Maulana Karenga, a teacher at California State University. The holiday is based on the customs and traditional values of the African people. The name Kwanzaa means "first fruits of the harvest" in Swahili.

The colors of Kwanzaa are red, black, and green. Red stands for the struggle of freedom. Black is the symbol of the African-American people. Green represents hope and the future of African-Americans.

A candle holder called a kinara holds seven candles, three red, one black and three green. Each evening one candle is lit to celebrate a special Kwanzaa principle. The seven principles of Kwanzaa are: unity, self-determination, collective work and responsibility, cooperative economics, purpose, creativity, and faith. Important Kwanzaa items include the mkeka (muh-**kāk**-uh), or mat; fruits and vegetables, including corn; the unity cup; candles; and the kinara.

Throughout Kwanzaa, families and friends gather and often exchange handmade gifts. The last day of Kwanzaa includes special food, music, and dancing.

Bookmark Gift

Things you will need

- Black and yellow construction paper
- Green and red ricrac
- White glue
- Scissors

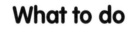

Happy Kwanzaa From Sabrina

What to do

1. Cut a 2" x 6" rectangle from black construction paper.

2. Cut a 1" flame shape from yellow construction paper and glue it to the top of the "candle."

3. Glue red and green ricrac around all edges of the bookmark and allow to dry.

4. Write your name on the bookmark.

5. If desired, give it as a Kwanzaa gift.

Weave a Mkeka

Things you will need
- Red, black, and green construction paper
- Ruler
- Clear contact paper, optional
- Clear tape
- Scissors

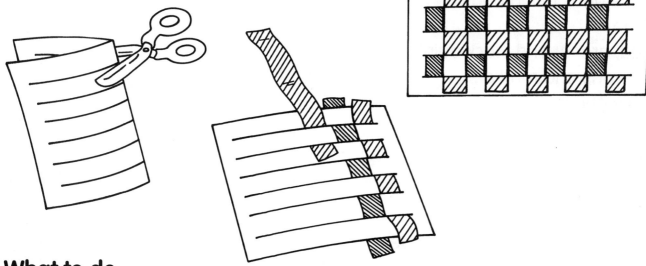

What to do

*   Teacher: Prepare the following for the student: fold one piece of 9" x 12" black construction paper in half lengthwise and make cuts into the paper beginning at the fold and ending about 1" from the edge (see diagram).

*   Cut five 1" x 12" strips from red construction paper, and four strips from green construction paper.

*   Show the student how to weave the strips over and under the cuts in the paper.

1. Weave the mkeka.

2. When the weaving is complete, tape the ends of the construction paper strips in place.

3. If desired, laminate the mkeka or cover with clear contact paper for protection.

Fruit Print Banner

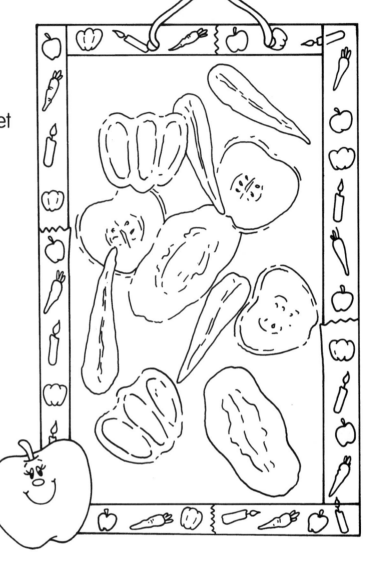

Things you will need

- Brown paper grocery bag
- White construction paper
- Fruits and vegetables (carrot, sweet potato, apple, bell pepper, etc.)
- Knife and cutting board
- Glue
- Red, green, and black paint
- Crayons and markers
- Hole punch
- Twine
- Scissors

What to do

* Teacher: Before beginning, use a knife to cut the fruits and vegetables in half.

1. Cut strips of brown paper bag to frame a piece of construction paper.

2. Decorate the brown paper strips with Kwanzaa items, such as candles, fruits, vegetables, etc. Then, glue the strips around the construction paper.

3. Dip a fruit or vegetable in red, black, or green paint and press it onto the construction paper.

4. Continue until the banner is filled.

5. Allow the banner to dry.

6. Punch two holes near the top of the banner and string with twine for hanging.

RAMADAN

Ramadan is an important holy month for Muslims because it is the month in which the Koran, the holy book of Islam, was revealed to the prophet Muhammad. Ramadan is the ninth month of the Islamic year and falls at different times of the year because it is based on cycles of the moon.

During the month of Ramadan, Muslims may not eat or drink during daylight hours, but can eat between sunrise and sunset. The observance of the fast is one of the five chief religious duties of a Muslim. Muslims also recite the Koran and say special prayers during Ramadan.

When the new moon comes, Ramadan is over. To celebrate successful fasting, Muslims have a festival called Eid ul Fitr. Family and friends gather together wearing new clothes and enjoy feasting and exchanging gifts. They wish each other "Eid Mubarak," a greeting which means "Have a happy and blessed Eid!"

Crescent and Star Cookies

Things you will need

- Refrigerated sugar cookie dough
- Star and crescent shaped cookie cutters
- Rolling pin
- Cookie sheet

What to do

* Teacher Note: Although the crescent and star have no religious significance, the symbols are popularly associated with mosques and Islam.

* Roll the dough on a clean, flat surface.

1. Allow each child to press one cookie cutter into the dough.

2. Place the cookies on a cookie sheet and bake following the package directions.

3. Enjoy the cookies as a snack.

Mosque

What to do

* Enlarge the mosque patterns on construction paper.

1. Cut out the patterns.

2. Glue the pieces together on construction paper (see diagram).

3. Color the mosque with crayons or markers.

4. Spread glue over the dome shapes of the mosque and sprinkle the glue with colored glitter.

Things you will need

- Mosque patterns (below)
- Construction paper
- Crayons and markers
- Colored glitter
- Glue
- Scissors

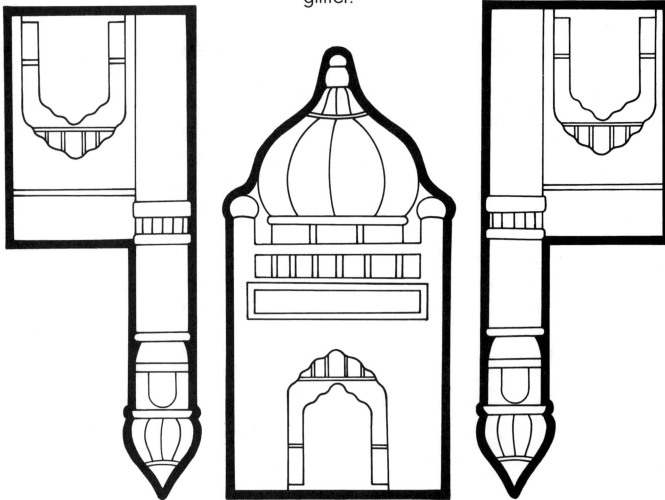